BEAUTIFUL ORTHODOXY

THE GOODNESS, ~~,~~ AND BEAUTY
OF LIFE ~~~~ CHRIST

MARK GALLI

Cover: *Grace Remains—Nard* by Makoto Fujimura
73x91 cm, mineral pigments, gold on kumohada paper
stretched over canvas, 2016

BEAUTIFUL ORTHODOXY

TABLE OF CONTENTS

FOREWORD

In the beginning was the Word, and the Word was with God, and the Word was God. In him was life, and that life was the light of all mankind. The light shines in the darkness, and the darkness has not overcome it.
—John 1:1, 4–5 (NIV)

 probably don't need to tell anyone reading this foreward that we live in an angry, at times ugly, increasingly more confused world. The tone of our rhetoric—across all media and even behind some closed church doors—is more rage than redemption.

Is more disgrace than grace.

You've seen it! You've heard it yourselves! On websites where attacking individuals and movements is second nature; and on Twitter, where shameless epithets leave helpless targets shamed and scarred for life. Even *Time* magazine felt compelled to feature this downward-digital-spiral in its August 29, 2016, cover story, "Why We're Losing the

Internet to a Culture of Hate."

A season of disrespect defines our so-called enlightened age. And making matters eternally worse, the truth of our convictions—the truth of God's Truth—seems increasingly worn down by attractive heresies and ugly orthodoxies that in the end are destined to leave more and more of God's creation in despair and without a sense of hope.

Fewer people, including those raised in the church, consider biblical Christianity as a viable worldview that can help individuals and cultures flourish.

This is darkness.

But taking our cues from the apostle John's opening lines of his mighty gospel prologue, we know Christ's light still shines in the darkness. Underscore: Shines right now in the darkness. And the darkness has not, cannot, will not, overcome it.

We need to meditate on this profound truth and let it overwhelm and overcome all of the anxieties today's media frenzy sow on a daily basis. We then need to be the church and collectively reflect the true light of Christ back onto this age of anger and confusion.

As his redeemed body, we can and must live what we at Christianity Today are calling Beautiful Orthodoxy: an orthodoxy anchored firmly on our risen Christ and his gospel, and expressed not with screams of our own self-righteousness but in a language and with lives that model the unconditional love and bloodstained beauty of our Lord Jesus Christ.

Early church fathers like St. Augustine wrote that truth expressed without beauty, without love, without hope was no Truth at all. But when lived faithfully and fearlessly, Beautiful Orthodoxy boldly demonstrates for all how the Truth that sets us free—our orthodoxy—can result in freedom and flourishing not only for the church but for all those communities and cultures the church intersects.

As president and CEO of Christianity Today, I've been blessed to see Beautiful Orthodoxy expressed in word and deed all across North America and around the world. In this regard, two quick "for instances" come immediately to mind.

The first concerns my friend and kingdom coworker Albert Reyes. He is the former president of Baptist University of the Americas in San Antonio and current CEO of Buckner International. He recently spoke regarding the call of the burgeoning Latino church in North, Central, and South America. "Latino evangelical Christians," he said, "will be more interested in the welfare of the community at large than their own personal welfare. Hispanics will help evangelical congregations gravitate toward a balanced application of the gospel to include issues of social justice and equality for everyone in the community."

The balance my brother is talking about for this piece of God's kingdom speaks of the gospel-grounded conviction and Christ-centered love that is Beautiful Orthodoxy. Truth immersed in beauty that brings flourishing and results in hope.

I'm seeing the same hope in churches that extend grace to the record number of ex-offenders desperately wanting a new life.

"If we do not welcome the prisoner, or anyone else who is a sinner in need of the grace found in Jesus, we are resisting the Holy Spirit," said Marco David, pastor of Midwest Bible Church in Chicago. "Pastor Jim Cymbala of the Brooklyn Tabernacle puts it this way: 'A church that is not fully open to all people, (despite their color, class, culture, crime, crisis) is not fully open to the Holy Spirit.'"

"At the root of our fear is a lack of our abounding in Christ's love (1 Thess. 3:12; Phil. 1:9)," Marco continues. "Love conquers all, including fear. Love compels us to take risk, to show compassion, and to extend grace to the undeserving and the unloved (2 Cor. 5:14). If our love is not extended to the ex-offender, we are more like a social club than a church. We must increase in love. We must pray radically to love radically."

And to underscore his point, Pastor Marco recently started an evening program where ex-offenders and their families—along with church members—gather for a meal, a time of worship and Bible study, and, most of all, prayer. Out of this regularly come a number of "new creations."

Conviction and love. The twin pillars upon which evangelist Billy Graham built Christianity Today back in 1956. Today we call it Beautiful Orthodoxy.

Now is the time, in the words of New York pastor Tim Keller, to be a "counterculture for the common good."

Now is the time to model Beautiful Orthodoxy in our evangelism and in how we bring gospel conviction and Christ's love to bear on individual lives, on our communities, and on the demanding and all-too-divisive issues of our day—issues like immigration, incarceration, mental health, hunger, poverty, justice, and so on.

In a world in desperate need of truth, goodness, and beauty, we have the privilege of communicating the breadth of the true, good, and beautiful Gospel in our words, in our actions, and in our lives.

And in doing so, we can attest the plausibility of the Christian faith in the minds and hearts of our culture. Or paraphrasing Charles Taylor: We can help those who dare to believe, to believe. And we can help those who believe, to live.

"I came," Jesus said in John 10:10, "so that they can have real and eternal life, more and better life than they ever dreamed of."

A Beautiful Orthodoxy indeed! And the reason this book is needed now more than ever.

—*Harold B. Smith*
President and CEO,
Christianity Today

INTRODUCTION

 2013 study of the Twitter-like network Weibo found that anger is the most influential emotion on social media. Beihang University researchers sifted through 70 million messages of the Chinese miniblog from a 6-month period, categorizing them by joy, sadness, anger, and disgust. They found that anger spread more widely than the other emotions and affected others as well. A writer concluded that "one angry post could negatively influence a follower of a follower of a follower."[1]

This study reflects not only the social media reality of China but also of the world. And it's not just confined to the Internet. All forms of media work to catechize us day in and day out to be angry. Edward Wasserman, an expert on ethics in news media, was quoted in *Scientific American* as saying, "Unfortunately, mainstream media have made a fortune teaching people the wrong ways to talk to each other, offering up Jerry Springer, Crossfire, Bill O'Reilly. People understandably conclude rage is the political vernacular, that this is how public ideas are talked about."[2]

Why so much anger about, well, everything? It spews forth at politicians who lie, at systems that discriminate, at businesses that exploit, at abortionists who murder, at pastors who fall, at police who kill, and at those who kill police—at injustices and wrongs whenever and wherever they manifest themselves. Anger and frustration are everywhere. We see them and feel them every day. But what exactly is driving all this?

Rabbi David Wolpe, in a recent article in *Time*, commented on a fall 2015 study that concluded Americans are angrier than ever. He says:

> Why are Americans so angry? All of us, of whatever group, live some version of the "Whig interpretation of history," a theory identified and criticized by the historian Herbert Butterfield almost a century ago that sees history as an ever-increasing march to enlightenment. If you believe that things should get better and better, then it is infuriating when they do not.[3]

Wolpe is on to something, but I believe the disappointment goes even deeper. It's not just that we're not making progress, it's that we have this unshakable sense that something has gone terribly wrong and it can't be fixed. Deep within, we believe that life should be good and true and beautiful, but it is far from it. When the information highway becomes the demolition derby, as it so often does, we strike out in frustration. And the more powerless we feel in the face of social injustice and the wrongs committed against us personally, the more anger makes a home in us. For some, it erupts in bursts of outrage, in the public square and private spaces. For others, it morphs into a quiet despair that they attempt to numb with a countless round of entertainments and shopping.

Christians believe that our longing for the good, the true, and the beautiful finds its completion in the Way, the Truth, and the Life, who is Jesus Christ. All hearts are restless and angry until they find their rest in the Son of God. But even we Christians have a hard time grasping and living into the fullness of this reality.

Some of us are captivated by Jesus Christ, and we grasp the liberating power of the great Christian doctrines and the wisdom of Christian ethics. But we become proud and self-satisfied that we've crossed our theological t's and dotted our moral i's, and we make sure other people know it. We lash out at the evils of our times, "speaking truth to power," being "prophetic" about "objective truth" and "traditional values." We inadvertently imply that God loves only those who believe and obey the truth, and we come across as smug and self-righteous. We too often have come to represent ugly orthodoxy.

Other Christians, in reaction, soften the gospel to make it more relevant and pleasing to the ear of a culture that so desperately wants to feel good about itself. We are quick to marginalize what we now derisively call "dogma" and question values that have stood the test of time. We explain that we live in a new time that requires new ethics. The last thing we want to do is make others feel uncomfortable for their choices. God, we say, accepts us just the way we are—in fact, he has created us that way. This path is the way of beautiful heresy.

These seemingly irreconcilable approaches have this in common: they both truncate the full gospel. They abandon one aspect of the full mystery we are called to live. They give up either orthodoxy or beauty, and in doing so, end up with a Jesus who is only half man and half God.

Jesus Christ is indeed the way and truth—all that we mean by "orthodoxy." We tend to use this word to describe what Christians believe, but the word is much richer. Better to think as do our brothers and sisters in the Eastern Orthodox tradition. For them, orthodoxy is a way of life grounded in truth, and truth that expresses itself in all of life. To be orthodox is to know the truths that set one free (the classic doctrines of the Christian faith) and to live out that freedom in daily life, with the values that have stood the test of time (classic Christian ethics).

Yet Jesus Christ is also the life. At one level, this means that he is the one who conquers death and offers life eternal to all. But as many biblical scholars have noted, "eternal life" in the Bible is not only about quantity (life that never ends); it is especially a life of unimaginable quality. There are many words that describe that quality, something for which anyone created in God's image instinctively yearns. One word that is especially relevant in our day was signaled by the famous existential psychologist Rollo May:

> Beauty is the experience that gives us a sense of joy and a sense of peace simultaneously. Other happenings give us joy and afterwards a peace, but in beauty these are the same experience. Beauty is serene and at the same time exhilarating; it increases one's sense of being alive.... Beauty is the mystery which enchants us. Like all higher experiences of being human, beauty is dynamic; its sense of repose, paradoxically, is never dead, and if it seems to be dead, it is no longer beauty.[4]

We are attracted to beauty precisely because it imbues life with transcendence. It fills us with joy and peace because it indirectly and mysteriously manifests the One who is the Life. One might paraphrase our Lord and say that Jesus Christ is the way, the truth, and the beautiful. Or to put it more succinctly, it is in Jesus Christ that we can know, relish, and live into "beautiful orthodoxy."

An integrated life in Jesus Christ does not abandon orthodoxy—the pursuit of truth and goodness. Neither does it forsake the beautiful— all that makes life extraordinary.

This book is an attempt to understand a little more deeply what it means to pursue a life of beautiful orthodoxy. It does so by examining what in philosophy are called the *transcendentals*: the good, the true, and the beautiful. These ideals are transcendent because they harken to ultimate, divine realities. The following chapters alternate between the common and uncommon expressions of these transcendentals—to show how we yearn for the good, the true, and the beautiful, yet how Jesus Christ transcends our usual understanding of these words.

We all strive to realize these ideals, even though we may not always be aware of them. It is these ideals that, when frustrated, cause us so much grief and anger, because we instinctively know life should be more than what we find ourselves embedded in. But rather than scold ourselves, let us view our anger charitably and recognize that it signals the frustration of our deepest longing: ultimately to know the One who fulfills them and promises to fill us with himself.

CHAPTER 1

COMMON GOOD

 here beats in the breast of every human being the desire to do good. We recognize early on in preschoolers, who—while often selfish and possessive—will suddenly and without prompting offer to share a cookie with a playmate. We see it in students pondering what they can do to make a difference with their lives. And in the mother nursing her baby in the middle of the night. And the father who pulls an extra shift to provide for his family. And the senator who votes his conscience though it might cost him an election. We can remember times we found ourselves embedded in a morally complex situation in which the good called to us to not do what is expedient but what is right. We have obeyed that call for no other reason than it was, in our eyes, the right thing to do.

Where does it come from, this strange and mysterious urging that sometimes prompts individuals to even give up their own lives for another? Why this compelling drive to do the right thing?

Some say this is an optimistic picture of human nature, especially today.

They argue that it is self-preservation that rules humankind, and that we live in a time when "everyone does what is right in his own eyes." People care more about satisfying their own desires and finding personal happiness than being good.

The daily headlines, replete with stories of greed, injustice, murder, and mayhem, are a singular witness to this view and a sure cure for optimism about the human race. So no, we mustn't be naive, especially about our own times. But such behavior is more or less what we've had to deal with since biblical times, when the phrase "everyone did what was right in his own eyes" sprung forth. The line comes from the Book of Judges, which describes an era of Israel's history before Saul established the monarchy. But what's interesting to note is that it does not describe immoral behavior as such—and even suggests some of the good that all human beings strive to realize.

Take the story of Micah, who stole 1,100 shekels of silver from his mother. He later regretted his theft and returned the silver. His mother was so grateful, she exclaimed, "The Lord bless you, my son!" This story starts by showing someone who actually did right in the end.

Then the mother said she would consecrate her silver "to the Lord" by having her son make an idol overlaid with some of the silver. Micah did so, and going even further, he created a shrine in his home to hold the images of their household gods, installing one of his sons as priest.

That's when the author of the story says, "In those days there was no king in Israel. Everyone did what was right in his own eyes" (Judges 17:6, ESV).

The story, then, illustrates religious decadence—the worship of idols—and not immorality as such. The son had confessed his thievery, returned the stolen goods, and then honored his mother's wishes. Even in an age of religious confusion, then, when idols abound, people still wanted to do the right thing.

This ancient story is a picture of the confusions that swirl around us today. Many rightly fret about the moral collapse of the United States. The evidence is not hard to find. Take the state of marriage: from the number of couples who live together without making vows, to the depressing divorce statistics of those who do, to the definition of marriage itself. Yes, trends like this suggest deep moral confusion. But to be fair, it isn't as if we live in a time of moral anarchy. Married couples, and even those who live together, still believe in sexual fidelity. Except among a few outliers (like advocates of open marriage), most people believe adultery or sexual unfaithfulness to be a grave breach of the relationship.

We can add to that a host of other ideals we affirm: we think it wrong to lie, steal, or kill; to discriminate against anyone; to produce shoddy or dangerous products; to be cowardly; and so on. We do disagree, however, about how these ideals work themselves out in public life. For example, pro-choice advocates may not believe the child in the womb is technically a "person," but they do not advocate wanton killing of anyone they do consider a person.

To be sure, we fall short of our ethical ideals. In the evenings, we often think back over the day: we snapped impatiently at our children; we ignored something our supervisor asked us to do; we found ourselves resenting a homeless man seeking a handout; and so on. But we recognize these as shortcomings, and we strive to do better. We may fail to meet our ideals, but we don't deny them—even if it would be psychologically easier for us to do so. Instead, we try to respond to that mysterious inner call to do good, however we understand it.

THE GOOD LIFE DAY TO DAY

Over 20 years ago, a book by Robert Fulghum caught the public's imagination: *All I Really Need to Know I Learned in Kindergarten*. In the opening pages, he summarizes his thesis:

These are the things I learned [in kindergarten]:

Share everything.

Play fair.

Don't hit people.

Put things back where you found them. Clean up your own mess. Don't take things that aren't yours. Say you're sorry when you hurt somebody.

Wash your hands before you eat.

Flush.

Warm cookies and cold milk are good for you.

Live a balanced life—learn some and think some and draw and paint and sing and dance and play and work every day some.

Take a nap every afternoon.

When you go out into the world, watch out for traffic, hold hands, and stick together.

Wonder.

Remember the little seed in the Styrofoam cup. The roots go down and the plant goes up and nobody really knows how or why, but we are all like that. Goldfish and hamsters and white mice and even the little seed in the Styrofoam cup—they all die. So do we.

And then remember the Dick-and-Jane books and the first word you learned—the biggest word of all—LOOK.

Everything you need to know is in there somewhere. The

Golden Rule and love and basic sanitation. Ecology and politics and equality and sane living.[5]

This is Fulgham's summary of the good life. These sorts of lists pop up regularly. A less playful but equally earnest example comes from an Elite Daily article titled "How to Live the Good Life." It begins, "Living the good life can mean something different for everyone. However, there is still a general understanding as [to] what this idea entails to most human beings living in the modern world." It then lists 21 "simple ways to live the good life," which include "slow down," "foster and nurture relationships," "be self-sufficient," "assist others," "be spontaneous," "keep your promises," and "be here now."[6]

Such lists are today's Ten Commandments, though they veer from them in significant ways. Still, they make intuitive sense in our culture, which regularly reinforces these ideals. The CNN piece "5 Examples of Humans Being Amazing" tells the story of Vicki Thomas, a generous Miami-Dade police officer who helped a woman in need. Jessica Robles was penniless and needed food for her three children. Thomas caught Robles taking $300 worth of groceries from a store. She looked at Robles's criminal history on her cruiser's computer. Thomas didn't find any major charges, so instead taking her into custody, she issued Robles a notice to appear in court to answer for a misdemeanor.

Thomas also told Robles about food banks and church food pantries—and then escorted her back into the store and bought her some groceries.

Thomas later said, "I made the decision to buy her some groceries because arresting her wasn't going to solve the problem with her children being hungry."[7]

Such stories inspire us to "assist others" when the opportunity presents itself.

Millennials are said to be "bad . . . at thinking and talking about moral issues." This is David Brooks's conclusion after studying an in-depth survey conducted by Notre Dame sociologist Christian Smith. "Smith and company asked about the young people's moral lives, and the results are depressing."[8]

Even if this generation struggles with how to think deeply about moral issues, Brooks still acknowledges that they hold to some morals. This is a cohort that is said to be less judgmental and more hesitant to proclaim their morality, the classic virtues of charity and humility. Socially, they are passionate about volunteer work, reducing carbon emissions, ethically produced products, and racial justice.

So yes, the picture is mixed, and we could pour forth many more examples of both selfishness and altruism. But even when we find ourselves doing what is right in our own eyes, we have an inner mysterious moral compass that pricks us when we live like that. That emotional and intellectual discomfort is called guilt and shame. It's the recognition that we have not only failed but have also failed someone or something—who or what we cannot always say. The equally unbidden prompting each morning to resolve to do better, to do what is right—that too is a mysterious reality that characterizes our daily existence.

A CURSE AND A BLESSING

These prompts make life harder. They complicate things. How much easier it would be to do what is right in our own eyes and be done with it. But we cannot *not* be affected by guilt and obligation, at least not for long.

In some ways this phenomenon is a curse. In his letter to Rome, the apostle Paul calls this moral struggle "wretched" (Rom. 7:24). But there is another sense in which it is blessed, which is alluded to at the beginning of our existence:

> So God created mankind in his own image,
> in the image of God he created them (Gen. 1:27)

This speaks to a deeper sense of who we are. For one, we are created. We are not an accident of an evolving universe. We have been the apple of the Creator's eye from "before the foundation of the world," who made us "to be holy and blameless before him in love" (Eph. 1:4, NRSV). We've been created with moral purpose. As hard as culture tries to erase the memory of that purpose, enticing us with its entertainments and degradations, that memory is permanently imprinted on our souls.

We not only have a creative purpose, but our being is shaped by the One in whose image—goodness and love—we've been created. Our being is true to its deepest self when we reflect the fullness of this image.

No wonder we cannot escape this inner moral compass. We can no more escape it than we can our beating hearts. To live is to be haunted by goodness and love—and, yes, to have a deep sense of failure that we have not always done what is good and loving.

But among the many good impulses we feel obligated to obey, what lies at the core? We want to do the good, but we are often confused about what that looks like. Some believe that sexual relations outside the commitment of marriage, or between persons of the same sex, are good. Others believe that taking the life of the unborn is justified. Still others believe that the good requires that we never make judgments about anyone's chosen behavior.

We each have come up with lists of behaviors we believe constitute the good life, but who says our list is right? Why adhere to one person's ideals rather than another one's?

Christians are freed from fashioning their own lists. Our beliefs about the good come not from our creative and moral imaginations, but from outside ourselves. We believe a good God has revealed himself to the world, first through the people of Israel and then supremely in Jesus Christ. He has not left us with vague feelings to do what is right, but with specific and concrete commands and examples.

The Bible contains some of the most succinct and beautiful expressions of the good, beginning with the Ten Commandments. Among other things, it forbids idolatry, killing, and stealing, and mandates honoring the Sabbath and one's parents.

Another summary is found in the Book of Micah: "He has shown you, O mortal, what is good. And what does the LORD require of you? To act justly and to love mercy and to walk humbly with your God" (6:8).

Despite its deserved reputation as a testament of grace, the New Testament also enjoins us to specific acts of goodness:

> Flee the evil desires of youth and pursue righteousness, faith, love, and peace, along with those who call on the Lord out of a pure heart. (2 Tim. 2:22)

> But the fruit of the Spirit is love, joy, peace, forbearance, kindness, goodness, faithfulness, gentleness, and self-control. (Gal. 5:22–23)

When it comes to the good, the Bible gets pretty specific at times. We are called to shun sexual immorality (1 Cor. 6:9) and to live chastely (Matt. 5:28). We are called to eschew selfish ambition and instead look after the interests of others first (Phil. 2:3–4). We are instructed to avoid greed (Col. 3:5) and instead give generously to the needy (2 Cor. 9:6–7). These are just a few of the specific biblical admonitions that go against the grain of our culture, where many people, in the name of the good, advocate the opposite.

To be sure, even Christians argue about the exact nature of the good, especially in matters of prudential judgment. Should our children be enrolled in public schools or be homeschooled? Is it okay to imbibe alcohol or is it better to abstain? But there is much more that we agree on, virtues and practices clearly enjoined in the Bible about which theologians have thought long and hard. It is no accident that the moral life has taken a certain shape century after century in the Christian church, in both the East and West.

'A PROFOUNDLY GOOD HUMAN BEING'

Despite the opposition of some hardcore secularists to the classic Christian virtues, these morals are still admired by most people in the world. Examples abound, but let us take just one: Nelson Mandela, the South African activist and former president.

His fight against the injustice of apartheid landed him in prison for nearly three decades. Neville Alexander, Mandela's fellow prisoner for 10 years, recalled:

> I was impressed mainly by the warmth and the genuine interest, which was a feature that, subsequently I discovered, is very much part of the man and something which I also must admit now, I learned from him . . . to give your full attention to your interlocutor, and really take notice of what people are saying, listen to them carefully. In his case, there was a spontaneous, charismatic exuding of warmth. That's probably the most important, most vivid memory I have of our first meeting.[9]

International pressure led to Mandela's release in 1990, after which he worked to eradicate apartheid. In 1994, he became the first black president of South Africa and formed a multiethnic government to oversee the country's transition. He worked for reconciliation, not vengeance, and negotiated a peaceful end to segregation while practicing forgiveness for the white government that had imprisoned him. He once said, "As I walked out the door toward the gate that would lead to my freedom, I knew if I didn't leave my bitterness and hatred behind, I'd still be in prison."

Kindness and compassion seemed to be written on his face. Jessie Duarte, Mandela's personal assistant for over three years, remarked about his humility, even after he was an international hero.

> He always made his own bed, no matter where we traveled. I remember we were in Shanghai, in a very fancy

hotel, and the Chinese hospitality requires that the person who cleans your room and provides you with your food, does exactly that. If you do it for yourself, it could even be regarded as an insult.

So in Shanghai I tried to say to him, "Please don't make your own bed, because there's this custom here." And he said, "Call them, bring them to me."

So I did. I asked the hotel manager to bring the ladies who would be cleaning the room, so that he could explain why he himself has to make his own bed, and that they not feel insulted. He didn't ever want to hurt people's feelings. He never really cared about what great big people [thought] of him, but he did care about what small people thought of him. That used to amaze me. He didn't mind if he insulted a very important person, or said something to them that was unkind, because he said they could fend and fight for themselves. But he would never insult someone who did not have power.[10]

Upon Mandela's death, President Barack Obama summed up the world's admiration for him: "we have lost one of the most influential, courageous, and profoundly good human beings that any of us will share time with on this Earth."[11]

We are not only internally prompted to do good, we are inspired when we see it in action. It is a beautiful thing to behold, and thus is part and parcel of what it means to pursue Beautiful Orthodoxy. Beautiful Orthodoxy is grounded in the revelation that we have been created in the image of a good God to live good lives.

That being said, as good as the good life is, upon deeper reflection, this mandate is ultimately not everything it's cracked up to be. As anyone who takes the good seriously knows, the pursuit of good, in and of itself, is a hazardous journey, fraught with dangers that we cannot avoid. We need something more than just common good.

CHAPTER 2

UNCOMMON GOOD

esus was approached one day by a desperate man, who fell before him and asked, "Good teacher, what must I do to inherit eternal life?"

In his words and tone, the man was showing respect to an admired religious figure. But surprisingly Jesus would have none of it. "'Why do you call me good?' Jesus answered. 'No one is good—except God alone'" (Mark 10:17–18).

This statement mystifies because we think of Jesus as a good person—in fact, the best person there ever was. But Jesus doesn't want to be thought of in this way. So he bluntly deflected the man's honorific description.

Jesus did this sort of thing time and again. For example, he began his public ministry by identifying with sinners, not with the good people of his day. He sojourned into the wilderness to hear a preacher who scolded sinners and baptized people that they might be forgiven. After listening to John the Baptist, Jesus submitted to being baptized.

What else would this communicate than that he was a sinner? The church has never believed that Jesus had sins that needed forgiving—John recognized that himself when he objected to baptizing Jesus. But when John balked, Jesus said, "[I]t is proper for us to do this to fulfill all righteousness" (Matt. 3:15). Jesus insisted that he wanted to be seen as one who at least bore sins.

Then there was the company he kept. Jesus was regularly accused by the righteous people of his day—the Pharisees—of cavorting with Jews who betrayed their country (helping Romans collect oppressive taxes) and with those who refused to follow the law. One scene occurred in the home of a Pharisee:

> When one of the Pharisees invited Jesus to have dinner with him, he went to the Pharisee's house and reclined at the table. A woman in that town who lived a sinful life learned that Jesus was eating at the Pharisee's house, so she came there with an alabaster jar of perfume. As she stood behind him at his feet weeping, she began to wet his feet with her tears. Then she wiped them with her hair, kissed them, and poured perfume on them.
>
> When the Pharisee who had invited him saw this, he said to himself, "If this man were a prophet, he would know who is touching him and what kind of woman she is—that she is a sinner." (Luke 7:36–39)

When Jesus traveled to Jericho, a tax collector named Zacchaeus climbed a tree to get a look at the famous teacher. When Jesus saw him, he called him to come down, saying, "I must stay at your house today" (Luke 19:5). Zacchaeus was thrilled, but the crowd was not: "All the people saw this and began to mutter, 'He has gone to be the guest of the sinner'" (Luke 19:7). So it's not just the righteous Pharisees who questioned his morality, but the common people as well.

Jesus also told stories in which he appeared indifferent to sin and unimpressed with righteousness. In the parable of the Prodigal Son, the sinful son is treated generously by the father, while the good son complains about being a mere afterthought (Luke 15).

In another parable, Jesus told the story of a king who prepares a wedding banquet. When his initial invitees reject his offer, the king tells his servants to go to street corners and invite anyone they can find. The servants do just that, and the wedding hall is filled with guests, "the bad as well as the good" (Matt. 22).

One of the great enigmas of Jesus is that while he is recognized as a great moral teacher, he appears uninterested in the life of virtue.

To be sure, Jesus never renounces the good. He tells the woman caught in adultery to "leave your life of sin" (John 8:11), and he befriends sinners that they might be saved (Luke 19:10). He also tells his followers that their righteousness must exceed even that of the moral exemplars of the day, the Pharisees (Matt. 5:20).

THE UNATTAINABLE GOOD LIFE

We begin to see a troubling paradox here, one that comes into play most forcefully in Jesus' Sermon on the Mount. This is where Jesus not only outlines the nature of the good life, but also raises the bar so high as to be out of reach of mere mortals. It is not only adultery that is proscribed, but lustful thoughts as well. It's not just murder that is forbidden, but also anger. We are to love our enemies and not resist an evil person. We are to practice spiritual disciplines humbly. We are not to store up riches on earth or to worry. We are, in summary, "to be perfect, even as your Father in heaven is perfect" (Matt. 5:48, NLT).

The Sermon on the Mount is universally hailed for its admirable principles. But to quote the disciples—after Jesus had announced another impossibility (the rich entering the kingdom of heaven): "Who then can be saved?" (Matt. 19:25). The disciples seemed to think that Jesus taught an ethic that is impossible to follow.

Commentators address this problem in many ways. One could write a book on just this theme.[12] An admittedly inadequate summary goes like this:

> Some argue that Jesus literally meant what he said. The problem is not with these teachings; the problem is with us. Jesus wouldn't have given these injunctions if he didn't think we could follow them. It's a matter of our willingness to obey them. Some qualify that by saying obedience is possible only with the power of the Spirit; others say this ethic can be realized only if practiced in the context of the Christian community. Others still say that, while not meant for every Christian, these sayings are the rule of life for those especially dedicated to Christ: priests, monks, and nuns, for example. The fact that no one in the 2,000 years since has been able to do so remains the most significant argument against the idea that the Sermon on the Mount can be lived with complete consistency.

> Others set the Sermon on the Mount in the context of Jesus' teaching about the kingdom of God. The Beatitudes and injunctions are illustrations of how Jesus should rule over every aspect of our lives. Or people say the Sermon on the Mount is not about how we behave but about discovering the love of God in Jesus and reflecting that love in the world.

Whatever our take, we're still left with massive frustration at our inability to live out the Sermon on the Mount. We're not good at letting Jesus rule over our entire lives or reflecting his love to the world.

That's why some have argued that this is the point: these injunctions are, at least in part, designed to frustrate and discourage us. They show us God's perfect will and, by implication, show how far we fall short. As Paul put it when referring the Old Testament law, "I found that the very commandment that was intended to bring life actually brought death" (Rom. 7:10). The same can be said about the Sermon on the Mount: it leads us to a hopelessness that only grace can heal.

This view has a long history, beginning with Romans 1 and 2, where Paul lays out his argument that all have sinned and fallen short of God's will. This is not just a biblical teaching but also a lived reality. We have tried, tried desperately to the point of tears, to obey the commands of Jesus, and we have failed time and time again. We have striven to bring justice to our community and nation and world, only to be thwarted time and again. If in fact the good life depends on perfect personal morality and social ethics, we are doomed.

But the gospel destroys that paradigm by announcing the most unexpected turn. God does not wait for us to live the godly and good life before pronouncing beatitudes over us; instead, God justifies the ungodly. Noted preacher-theologian Fleming Rutledge put it well:

> This differentiates Christian faith from religion in general, because religion in general has as its purpose to create godly people. Godliness is the goal. But twice, Paul refers to the justification of the ungodly, which is the most irreligious thing that's ever been said. It cuts against religion. We cannot achieve our own godliness. It must be given to us, and it has been given to us in this unrepeatable, world-overturning act of invasion of this satanic-occupied territory by the Son of God himself.[13]

God's mercy toward the ungodly changes the calculus of the good life. The criterion of *good* is not primarily about one's actions but one's demeanor. It's not concerned so much with excelling at ethics or religion but living with a deep sense that one is a failure in ethics and religion. One story Jesus tells drives this home:

> Two men went up to the temple to pray, one a Pharisee

and the other a tax collector. The Pharisee stood by himself and prayed: "God, I thank you that I am not like other people—robbers, evildoers, adulterers—or even like this tax collector. I fast twice a week and give a tenth of all I get."

But the tax collector stood at a distance. He would not even look up to heaven, but beat his breast and said, "God, have mercy on me, a sinner."

I tell you that this man, rather than the other, went home justified before God. For all those who exalt themselves will be humbled, and those who humble themselves will be exalted. (Luke 18:9–14)

The self-acknowledged failure to live up to God's law paradoxically cultivates a radical new way of conceiving of the good life. An incident in Jesus' life (John 8:1–11) illustrates this most powerfully.

A woman was caught in adultery, and the teachers of the law and the Pharisees dragged her before Jesus, who was teaching in the temple courts, surrounded by a crowd of people.

"Teacher, this woman was caught in the act of adultery," they told Jesus. "In the Law Moses commanded us to stone such women. Now what do you say?"

Jesus bent down and began writing something on the ground with his finger, saying nothing. But they kept badgering him.

What he said, after a seemly long pause, is one of the most memorable lines in history: "Let any one of you who is without sin be the first to throw a stone at her."

The woman's accusers slipped away one at a time until all were gone. Jesus stood up and asked the woman, "Where are they? Has no one condemned you?"

"No one, sir," she replied.

"Then," he said, "neither do I condemn you."

In that phrase, we see how we are to regard all whom we encounter day to day: "Neither do I condemn you."

In one way, the teachers of the law and the Pharisees represent the commandment that brings death. In a literal and concrete way, they wanted to use the law to kill this woman.

In another way, they represent God: though righteously angry about the gravity of sin, they finally do not condemn. It brings to mind the famous passage in Hosea, where God is pictured as incensed at the sinfulness of Israel and yet finally relents of his anger, saying,

> How can I give you up, Ephraim?
> How can I hand you over, Israel?
> How can I treat you like Admah?
> How can I make you like Zeboyim?
> My heart is changed within me;
> all my compassion is aroused.
> I will not carry out my fierce anger,
> nor will I devastate Ephraim again.
> For I am God, and not a man. (11:8–9)

The Pharisees and scribes were prodded into showing mercy to the woman because they recognized their own complicity in sin. God is merciful because he is God, and that is his nature—to be merciful.

> Who is a God like you,
> who pardons sin and forgives the transgression
> of the remnant of his inheritance?
> You do not stay angry forever
> but delight to show mercy. (Mic. 7:18)

A LIFE OF MERCY

It is no wonder, then, that in the end, the finest biblical picture of the good life is not a person who is morally righteous or religiously faithful, but one who practices mercy. This is precisely the logic Jesus used to explain his mission, why he spent time with ungodly people. To his critics, he quotes the prophet Hosea and says, "[G]o and learn what this means: 'I desire mercy, not sacrifice.' For I have not come to call the righteous, but sinners" (Matt. 9:13).

At this juncture, many rightly remind us that Jesus not only refused to condemn the adulterous woman but told her, "Go and sin no more" (John 8:11, NLT). And after Jesus' merciful encounter with the notorious tax collector, Zacchaeus was so moved that he vowed to reform. He told Jesus, "Look, Lord! Here and now I give half of my possessions to the poor, and if I have cheated anybody out of anything, I will pay back four times the amount" (Luke 19:8). And does not Micah's summary of the law—to do justice (6:8)—still apply? And despite its impossibility, shouldn't we still strive to live the Sermon on the Mount?

The paradigm of mercy says, "Of course!" The Bible never denies the value of morality. This is precisely the point Paul makes when describing the radical nature of grace—that God died for sinners and thus nullified their guilt and due judgment. He says, "What shall we say, then? Shall we go on sinning so that grace may increase? By no means! We are those who have died to sin; how can we live in it any longer?" (Rom. 6:1–2).

It's also why Paul normally ends his letters to churches by reminding his readers of what a moral life looks like. Christians often are confused about this, assuming that being merciful means we make no moral judgments whatsoever, and certainly not toward the person we are being merciful to. This is not mercy, but sentimentalism. Mercy treats the sinner with kindness and patience, but also—precisely because mercy wants the best for everyone—helps the immoral person see what new life in Christ looks like.

That being said, our moral lives are not motivated by the pursuit of virtue as much as by mercy. "Therefore, I urge you, brothers and sisters, *in view of God's mercy,* to offer your bodies as a living sacrifice" (Rom. 12:1, italics added). Paul regularly connects our moral lives to Jesus, the incarnation of mercy, exhorting us to "clothe" ourselves with Christ (Rom. 13:14) and to attain "the whole measure of the fullness of Christ" (Eph. 4:13). Peter comes at this similarly by reminding us that we are to "participate in the divine nature" (2 Pet. 1:4)—which of course is manifest in Jesus, who describes himself as "the way" (John 14:6).

While common morality is important, it is only penultimate. With effort, practice, and prayer, we can attain virtues that are part and parcel of a commonly understood good life. But by God's grace, we are called to more than that. This is why the parable of the Good Samaritan is commonly understood as the epitome of goodness. While the righteous and religious pass by the beaten man in the ditch, the Samaritan's response is summarized in one word: Who is the one who was a neighbor to the man? "The one who had mercy on him" (Luke 10:37).

Some wonder if mercy is just another virtue that cannot be perfectly fulfilled. And if so, we're back to square one: calling for a virtue that is impossible to fulfill and thus leaving us in despair. Not quite.

To be sure, we will never be perfectly merciful. But the "virtue" of mercy, if we need to call it that for a moment, has a self-correcting feature that actually prevents it from becoming just another moral injunction.

The life of mercy is grounded not in our virtue or even our striving for virtue, but in the fact that we are moral and religious failures. And thus the life of mercy begins not with vows to become moral heroes, but with repentance. The famous Jesus Prayer of the Eastern Orthodox tradition is a staple of its spirituality and the foundation of a life of mercy. It's fundamentally about repentance: "Lord Jesus Christ, son of God, have mercy on me, a sinner."

We see this posture in one well-known desert father, Sisoes. On his deathbed, after a lifetime of fervent prayer and asceticism, he told his brothers that he was seeing angels, but he was asking them to give him more time to repent.

His fellow monks were aghast and said, "You have no need for repentance."

But Sisoes replied, "I do not think that I have even begun to repent."[14]

The one who pursues a life of mercy never stops repenting, and lives and breathes "by the mercies of God" (Rom. 12:1, ESV). It does not surprise or discourage us when we discover we fail not only at goodness but also mercy. But an "ethic" of mercy is grounded in the reality that God is merciful to those who repent. The knowledge of God's persistent mercy in the face of our persistent failure makes room in our hearts to be merciful to ourselves—and just as important, merciful to others.

When those in places high and low inevitably and repeatedly fail and repent, our hearts, like God's, will grow warm with compassion. Instead of casting a stone, we'll be able to say, "Neither do I condemn you."

The penultimate good, the moral life, is good, even inspiring—up to a point. At that point, it reveals the unhappy reality of our failure in every dimension of life. That's when we see the ultimate good life, which comes from God and returns to God. Until the day we, and our communities, are made "holy and blameless before him in love" (Eph. 1:4, NRSV), we live from mercy to mercy. This too is a dimension of Beautiful Orthodoxy.

CHAPTER 3

COMMON TRUTH

n December 2015, a Wheaton College associate professor announced on Facebook that she was going to wear the hijab during the season of Advent to show solidarity with US Muslims. Muslims had been the subject of ugly remarks by public figures, so she wanted to do something symbolic to demonstrate Christian concern for them.

All seemed innocent enough to many, but the associate professor's action blew up in the media when she said she as a Christian was seeking solidarity with Muslims because, after all, "we worship the same God." In the ensuing controversy, many issues came into play, but theological truth was at the heart of it. Some vehemently denied that Christians and Muslims worship the same God. Some vehemently affirmed that we do. Others took a middle position: Yes, in a limited, philosophical sense, we worship the same God, the creator of heaven and earth. There is only one God, after all; but in deeper and more significant ways, we do not worship the same God, which in fact nearly all Muslims and Christians readily acknowledge.

This debate suggests that despite talk of this being a postmodern age, when truth is said to take a back seat, people remain passionate about truth, especially truth about God. The ardent pursuit of truth is not going away any time soon.

We care about truth in many spheres, in fact. We care about scientific truth, especially when it concerns our safety or health. We want to know the truth about the chemicals and ingredients in our food, the medicines in our bottles, and the safety features in our cars.

We also want our civic and church leaders to speak the truth. We are furious when they claim to be pursuing one course of action when in fact they surreptitiously are doing the opposite.

We want our loved ones to tell us the truth. A family or friendship can hardly flourish if we lie to one another.

We also want to know the truth about ourselves. We spend much of our lives trying to figure out who we are and what we are called to do.

And yes, we care especially about the truth that transcends all these concerns, the truth about the meaning and purpose of life, the truth about the God who is said to rule over heaven and earth. Who is this God? What is this God like? Why did he create the universe, our world, and humankind? What difference do answers to those questions make?

Enter *theology* and *doctrine*. Unfortunately these, along with *dogma*, have become dirty words to many, especially if we're talking about Christian doctrine, which is grounded in revelation. Thomas Paine's screed in *The Age of Reason* is perhaps the most famous example:

> The most detestable wickedness, the most horrid cruelties, and the greatest miseries that have afflicted the human race, have had their origin in this thing called revelation or revealed religion. It has been the most dishonorable belief against the character of the divinity, the most destructive to morality and the peace and

happiness of man, that ever was propagated since man
began to exist.[15]

Today, we hear public intellectuals, like the late Christopher Hitchens, speak along the same lines: "I find something repulsive in the
idea of vicarious redemption.... [T]he whole apparatus of absolution
and forgiveness strikes me as positively immoral, while the concept of
revealed truth degrades the whole concept of the free intelligence by
purportedly relieving us of the hard task of working out ethical principles for ourselves."[16]

It's not just Christian doctrine that is under assault, but doctrine in
general, because to believe in doctrine today is to be "dogmatic." A
perfect example is found in an article from *Psychology Today*, where
the author purports to show the difference between "Dogmatic and
Spiritual Religion":

> Dogmatically religious people are those who think that
> they're right and everyone else is wrong. For them, reli-
> gion isn't about self-development or experiencing the
> transcendent, but about adhering to a set of rigid beliefs
> and following the rules laid down by religious authori-
> ties. It's about defending their beliefs against anyone who
> questions them, asserting their "truth" over other peo-
> ple's, and spreading those beliefs to others. For them, the
> fact that other people have different beliefs is an affront,
> since it implies the possibility that their own beliefs may
> not be true. They need to convince other people that
> they're wrong to prove to themselves that they're right.

The author attributes such boorish behavior to "a fundamental anxi-
ety" that is "caused by our sense of being distinct individuals, existing
in separation to other people." Consequently, "we need to 'bolster'
our sense of self, to strengthen our identity. And religion, and other
belief systems, helps us to do this." In short, "[i]t encourages people
to withdraw empathy and morality from other groups, to see them as
inferior and ignorant."

Spiritual religion, on the other hand,

> promotes the higher attributes of human nature, like
> altruism and compassion, and fosters a sense of the
> sacred and sublime. "Spiritually religious" people . . .
> usually aren't evangelical; their attitude is that different
> religions are suited to different people, and that all reli-
> gions are different manifestations or expressions of the
> same essential truths.[17]

The author fails to recognize that it is doctrine that tells us that we
needn't fuss over our identity, because we are one in Christ; doctrine
further instructs us to love our neighbor in empathy and practical ser-
vice. The author cannot grasp that statements like "all religions are
different manifestations or expressions of the same essential truths"
is, in fact, a doctrine (that he asserts dogmatically, by the way).

THE TRUTHS WE LIVE BY

The question is not whether we should believe in doctrines or not
(because we already believe in them by default), but rather, which ones
do we believe? We want to believe in doctrines that, as best as they are
able, correspond to lived and ultimate reality. That is, we want our
doctrines to be true.

Orthodoxy is a word Christians use to suggest a set of beliefs that, taken
together, best reflect reality. One classic way those beliefs are succinctly
expressed in the West is in the words of the Nicene Creed:

> We believe in one God,
> the Father, the Almighty,
> maker of heaven and earth,
> of all that is, seen and unseen.
>
> We believe in one Lord, Jesus Christ,

the only Son of God,
eternally begotten of the Father,
God from God, Light from Light,
true God from true God,
begotten, not made,
of one Being with the Father.
Through him all things were made.

For us and for our salvation
he came down from heaven:
by the power of the Holy Spirit
he became incarnate from the Virgin Mary,
and was made man.

For our sake he was crucified under Pontius Pilate;
he suffered death and was buried.
On the third day he rose again
in accordance with the Scriptures;
he ascended into heaven
and is seated at the right hand of the Father.

He will come again in glory to judge the living and the dead,
and his kingdom will have no end.

We believe in the Holy Spirit, the Lord, the giver of life,
who proceeds from the Father and the Son.
With the Father and the Son he is worshiped and glorified.
He has spoken through the Prophets.
We believe in one holy catholic and apostolic Church.
We acknowledge one baptism for the forgiveness of sins.
We look for the resurrection of the dead,
and the life of the world to come.

The Nicene Creed does not include every important Christian belief (for example, it doesn't talk about the authority of Scripture, the exact nature of the Atonement, or justification by faith, among other things). And though the East and West differ on one line about the Holy Spirit,

Christians recognize this as "core Christianity"—those doctrines that outline the Christian's take on the deepest realities of the universe, the most profound truths.

For example, the Nicene Creed tells us that God is ultimately responsible for the universe. No matter that scientists estimate it's at least 3.5 billion years old, or that it is difficult to discern precisely how God started it, or if and when he has intervened in its history. The bottom line is this: the universe has its origin in God and is providentially ruled by God.

And not just any God, but a benevolent one, and one who is remarkably benevolent at that. He manifested himself in the person of Jesus Christ, who though he was "made man" is nonetheless "God from God." The creed does not explore the problem that God in Christ was trying to solve—it has no teaching about sin. It just assumes that we needed saving from something catastrophic: "for us and our salvation he came down from heaven." The creed assumes that salvation was accomplished by Jesus in that he became incarnate, that he "was crucified," that he "rose" from the dead, and that he "ascended into heaven." And the creed assures us that history is coming to a beatific end: We can look forward to "the resurrection of the dead, and the life of the world to come."

This God is not only remarkably benevolent but mysteriously complex: he is not only identified as Father and Son but also Holy Spirit, "the Lord, the giver of life," which sounds much like the "maker of heaven and earth" at the beginning of the creed. And on it goes. Each line helps fill out a remarkable story that stands at the heart of reality.

LIVING TRUTH, DAY BY DAY

One of our jobs as Christians is to live into these truths by being faithful to their spirit. God was humbly merciful by giving himself to us in Christ. To live truthfully means we do not merely acknowledge this truth in our minds but also in our actions. We seek to be humble and merciful to others, we strive to love our neighbors. We do this not merely because God commands us to love and be merciful; instead, he commands us to love and be merciful because the ultimate reality of the universe is love and mercy (namely, God), and only when we live in these ways do our lives correspond with the deepest realities.

A crucial task we face is not only to live the truth but also to teach and proclaim it in our time, for each age suffers from unique confusions.

Two particularly controversial issues illustrate this. First, we see a great deal of confusion today about what it means to be a human being, and this is manifested in debates about sexuality. There is a powerful strain in our society that assumes that the body does not tell us anything about what it means to be human. Some believe that one can be born with a male body while actually being a female. It's widely assumed that one's sexual organs have no bearing on the sexual partners one should pursue. Second, we move the discussion to the womb, and the assumption takes this form: the value of what is growing in the womb is not determined by its biological, physical status—which is clearly that of a human being—but by one's will. If I will this being to be born, it is valuable; if I don't will it, I can abort it. The value is in my mind.

For the Christian, such a worldview is not truthful; it doesn't accord with life's deepest realities. Those realities begin with the understanding that God created us as bodily creatures: "male and female he created them," whose distinctive bodily existence is designed that they might "[b]e fruitful and multiply" (Gen. 1:27–28). God confirmed that matter matters, that bodily existence is the blessed essence of our being, when he "became flesh and dwelt among us" (John 1:14, ESV), dying for us in the body, and rising for us in the body.

We don't decide from one day to the next whether the body is an essential part of who we are. It's woven into the fabric of the universe that we are, by God's design and incarnation, bodily creatures. That embodiment tells us a great deal of how we are to live with and respect the bodily existence of others. In short, we affirm traditional, biblical, sexual morality and protect life in the womb because we believe that doing so helps us align our lives to ultimate realities.

This does not mean we deny the complexities involved in addressing issues of the body. We cannot simply tell a man who feels like a woman or who is only sexually attracted to males to snap out of it and act like a man. We can't piously encourage a desperately impoverished pregnant woman to just trust God and have the baby. Our doctrine of the body prompts us to treat other embodied humans, no matter their confusion, temptation, or sin, with the compassion with which God has treated us. We should be bodily present and suffering with those who suffer, and we should wisely use our minds and bodies to seek ways to alleviate suffering and confusion.

Moving beyond hot-button topics, doctrine informs us about a whole host of issues we confront today. We care about creation not because creation is sacred, as some would have it, but because the Sacred created it and calls us to steward it wisely. The Christian view is grounded in the real difference between God and creation while believing they nonetheless have something to do with one another.

The poor and oppressed matter because those who find themselves particularly marginalized are people of particular concern to God. It is while we were enslaved by the powers of darkness that Christ came to liberate us. How much more should we seek to help liberate our brothers and sisters enslaved to the darkness of political and social oppression! Such a life corresponds to deep reality, and thus is lived truthfully.

So Christians are called to defend and proclaim the true, which means in large part, grounding ourselves in the particular truths of the gospel, that is, doctrine. It's part and parcel of the beautifully orthodox life. But as we will discover in the next chapter, this too is only penultimate truth, which like penultimate goodness, is also transcended by Jesus Christ.

CHAPTER 4

UNCOMMON TRUTH

ust as Jesus shows relatively little interest in penultimate good, so he also shows little interest in truth as doctrine, that is, truth in the abstract.

When standing before Pilate, he tells the governor, "[T]he reason I was born and came into the world is to testify to the truth. Everyone on the side of truth listens to me."

To this, Pilate famously replies, "What is truth?" (John 18:37–38). If Pilate had been paying attention to Jesus during his ministry, he would have known the answer.

Anyone familiar with John's gospel recognizes that Pilate's question drips with irony. No Gospel—no book in the New Testament, for that matter—tackles the theme of truth in-depth as does John's gospel. It begins with the twin affirmations that the Son comes from the Father "full of grace and truth" (1:14) and that, in contrast to Moses, who gave the law, Jesus Christ brings "grace and truth" (1:17).

What *truth* means is slowly unveiled in the Gospel. At moments, Jesus seems to use it in the penultimate sense: *truth* amounts to the trustworthy teachings about God and God's will. In one argument with the Pharisees, Jesus says, "[Y]ou are looking for a way to kill me, a man who has told you the truth that I heard from God" (8:40) and "[B]ecause I tell the truth, you do not believe me! Can any of you prove me guilty of sin? If I am telling the truth, why don't you believe me?" (8:45–46).

But even in this scene, Jesus uses the word *truth* in a way that suggests a deeper meaning. The argument begins when Jesus says, "If you hold to my teaching, you are really my disciples. Then you will know the truth, and the truth will set you free" (8:31–32). This can be understood to mean that Jesus teaches about ultimate truth. If we absorb his teachings, our intellectual moral horizons will expand, freeing us from restricting dogmas and leading us to human flourishing.

Many colleges and universities—like Johns Hopkins University and the California Institute of Technology—have adopted the latter part of the phrase "the truth will set you free" as their school motto with just this in mind. But of course in separating the last part from the first, they do violence to the fullness of what Jesus was saying. Jesus is seldom interested in abstract truth, the truth of propositions and teachings, the truth of doctrine or philosophical speculation or scientific investigation. Yes, he uses "truth" to mean his "teachings," but he links these teachings less with ideas than with his own person. He speaks of "his" teachings, and his teachings are unique not merely because he knows something *about* God and God's will.

His teachings are not to be simply acknowledged and believed, which is the usual way we respond to something taught. Instead, Jesus expects his followers to "hold" to them. What Jesus means by that is made clearer in John 15, for the Greek word translated as "hold" here is *meno*, the same word translated as "abide" (ESV). This is where Jesus reveals the difference between religious teachers and himself: "Abide in me, and I in you. As the branch cannot bear fruit by itself, unless it abides in the vine, neither can you, unless you abide in me" (15:4).

Bearing fruit—or human flourishing—does not come from grasping intellectual insights about the nature of reality, but by entering into and remaining in a personal, intimate, mystical relationship with Jesus Christ. We *abide* in his person, and he *abides* in ours. For Jesus, *truth* certainly includes believing in certain truths, certain teachings, certain doctrines about ultimate reality. But that is truth as milk. The meat of truth is not a concept but a person.

ULTIMATE TRUTH

This of course is said most succinctly and powerfully in one of the more well-known sayings of Jesus: "I am the way, the truth, and the life" (John 14:6). Jesus does not merely speak the truth, or lead us into truth, or point to the truth—he *is* the truth.

For Jesus, truth is not discerned through strict rules of logic. Truth is first and foremost connected with him. "Everyone on the side of truth listens to me" (John 18:37). In a philosophical discussion of truth, this would be nothing but arrogance, because the statement assumes that truth is not something out there that through vigorous discussion we grasp, however partially. Instead, to listen to Jesus is to grasp truth.

This truth is not just related to Jesus, but is also personal. Jesus drives this home in his statements about the indwelling Spirit of God:

> But when he, the Spirit of truth, comes, he will guide you into all the truth. He will not speak on his own; he will speak only what he hears, and he will tell you what is yet to come. He will glorify me because it is from me that he will receive what he will make known to you. (John 16:13–14)

Jesus' logic, as it were, is inexorable. Truth is so personal it dwells within us in the Holy Spirit. The Holy Spirit is not a figure of speech for humanity's creativity but the "Spirit of truth," a truth that the Spirit receives by way of hearing from another, namely what Jesus makes known to him. In having access to the indwelling Spirit of God, we have immediate access to Jesus, the truth.

The Holy Spirit has no other role than to reveal Jesus the Truth to us: "When the Advocate comes, whom I will send to you from the Father—the Spirit of truth who goes out from the Father—he will testify about me" (John 15:26).

Thus the truth of God, while embracing doctrine and theology, is first and foremost about *knowing* God. It is not a matter of knowing something about God but of "having God in oneself,"[18] as Gregory of Nyssa put it. The great church father also said that "no one can know God if it is not God who teaches him" and "there is no other way of knowing God than to live in him."

It's not unlike the difference between how an online algorithm knows us and how a spouse knows us. The more we shop at Amazon.com, the more the software knows what we're interested in buying. We are amazed (and annoyed) that, after looking at lamps online, advertisements for lamps appear on websites we subsequently visit. The program that tracks our searches knows a great deal about us, but is ultimately ignorant about us. Any person who knows us knows that, soon after our first search, we had already purchased a lamp, and thus we didn't need any more advertisements for them.

Similarly, we are tempted to pursue our knowledge of truth like computer programmers, looking for patterns in the behavior of God, and then deducing the truth about him. This can elicit some sense of the truth of God—but nothing like knowing the Truth personally.

This helps us more deeply appreciate the practical import of John's assertion that Jesus is full of "grace and truth."

SEEKING THE TRUE ONE

Anyone who has studied philosophy or theology in graduate school knows the problem with the pursuit of truth: the temptation to pride and arrogance. These vices often become embedded in the heart and mind of the maturing scholar. This is only natural, since students are taught to think critically, to challenge others' ideas, and to offer superior arguments. Fortunately, this is usually only a stage endured by younger scholars. But when truth is pursued as it is in graduate school, it is difficult to do so with grace. It is for this reason that Paul, a man who knew a thing or two about knowledge, characterizes this sort of enterprise as: "knowledge puffs up" (1 Cor. 8:1).

If one wants to pursue the truth of Jesus, the first step is not to engage in intellectual analysis, or to exploit logical weaknesses, or to display one's superior intellect. It begins not with argument to determine truth but with submission to the One who is truth.

John talks about this dynamic early in his Gospel: "The true light that gives light to everyone was coming into the world" (1:9). The truth is not something we seek out as much as something that seeks out us.

Furthermore, truth is not something we deduce but something we receive: "He came to that which was his own, but his own did not receive him. Yet to all who did receive him, to those who believed in his name, he gave the right to become children of God (1:11–12).

And to drive home the point of the ultrapersonal and humble reception of truth in Christ, John describes the disciples of Jesus like this: "children born not of natural descent, nor of human decision or a husband's will, but born of God" (1:13).

Jesus employs the analogy to human birth in his conversation with Nicodemus, saying to him, "You must be born again." The birth metaphor emphasizes our relative passivity in entering into a relationship with Jesus the Truth. We have no say regarding our natural birth, other than to accept it and live our lives, or to reject it, by taking our lives.

As Jesus put it, "For God so loved the world that he gave his one and only Son, that whoever believes in him shall not perish but have eternal life" (3:16).

In sum, truth, like the good, has two dimensions. Penultimate truth remains, like penultimate good, a worthwhile pursuit, one encouraged in the Bible from cover to cover. This sort of truth gives us the great teachings and doctrines by which we order our life together as Christians.

But there is a truth that transcends penultimate truth—in fact it is a truth of a different order. It not only makes penultimate truth possible. It changes the nature of what we normally mean by truth, moving it from merely right ideas to also include a right relationship with Truth himself.

CHAPTER 5

COMMON BEAUTY

 uger, the abbot of Saint-Denis in Paris, was in some ways a worldly man. He lived in the tumultuous high Middle Ages (1081–1151) and served in the courts of Pope Gelasius II and Calixtus II. He accompanied Louis VII when he traveled to marry Eleanor of Aquitaine, who would become one of the most powerful women of that era. Suger even served as a regent in the kingdom for a few years. He did not care for the Second Crusade, but preached about a new crusade toward the end of his life.

So he knew something about the ugliness of high politics, which is why he also appreciated beauty when he saw it. And Suger saw it mostly in church buildings, that is "the beauty of the house of God." He once waxed eloquent about "the loveliness of the many-colored stones" that "called me away from external cares." As he meditated on the towers exalting themselves into heaven, and the expansive interior flooded with light beaming through stained glass, he was transported from the material to the immaterial:

> then it seems to me that I see myself dwelling, as it were, in some strange region of the universe which neither exists entirely in the slime of earth nor entirely in the purity of heaven; and that, by the grace of God, I can be transported from this inferior to that higher world[19]

Suger was a leading patron of what became known as Gothic architecture. Its characteristics include the pointed arch, the ribbed vault, and the flying buttresses, as well as soaring towers and expansive interiors flooded with light. The eastern end of the Basilica Church of Saint-Denis, built by Abbot Suger and completed in 1144, is often cited as the first truly Gothic building. It is the architecture of many of the great cathedrals, abbeys, and churches of Europe.

Gothic architecture is one of the many ways beauty is manifested in our world. And the reaction of Suger is not uncommon: when we behold something beautiful, we start thinking about God. This is no doubt one reason Paul wrote, "[W]hatever is lovely, whatever is admirable—if anything is excellent or praiseworthy—think about such things" (Phil. 4:8). It is the biblical manifesto for beauty.

But when we talk about beauty, what exactly are we talking about? This chapter and the next were the most difficult to write precisely because the concept of beauty is elusive, not easily defined in words.

DEFINING BEAUTY

Beauty is to some degree relative to one's historical and cultural situation. People in different times and places employ different standards of beauty—thus the proverb, "Beauty is in the eye of the beholder." Perhaps this is why dictionaries tend to define beauty not by what it is in itself, but by what a beautiful object does to us, how it makes us feel: "the quality or aggregate of qualities in a person or thing that gives pleasure to the senses or pleasurably exalts the mind or spirit: loveliness."[20]

Then again, as many philosophers point out, if beauty is merely subjective, then the word has no meaning. It's merely a description of how we feel and says nothing about the object itself. One could then argue that if watching an animal being tortured gives me pleasure, it must be beautiful in some way. This will not do.

On the other hand, there are things nearly everyone calls beautiful, like a rose or a sunset. Our judgments are either mere coincidence, or in addition to our subjective sense, there is something objective about beauty. Thomas Aquinas argued therefore that beauty has certain characteristics: integrity, proportion, and clarity (that is, luminosity). A piece of art is said to possess integrity if it is whole (it hasn't been cut in parts), has proportion (if the various parts are in proper relation to one another), and is clear (has adequate light to reveal the beautiful). One can immediately see that this does not quite get at beauty—or that we're beginning to talk in circles.

As I said, beauty is elusive.

Today's art world has been deeply influenced by Georg Friedrich Hegel and those who exult creativity, spontaneity, and originality. These have become the criteria for what constitutes "art," and thus in some ways, beauty. The word *beauty* itself has become suspect because of its subjectivity, and has often been replaced with appreciation for merely the new and innovative. Thus a Campbell's soup can painting or a canvas painted in one solid color becomes art in part because no one had thought of doing it before.

I will therefore not walk through this thorny philosophical ground but simply take a common sense approach: there are things that most people in most times use the word *beautiful* to describe. While they are speaking about things that give them pleasure, they seem to be talking about things that have beauty in themselves. This is certainly the assumption of Scripture.

Beauty encompasses more than what the eyes see, of course. Music can be beautiful, as can the soft touch of a lover. But when the Bible talks about beauty, it usually refers to things or people we can see.

Two biblical women in particular are said to have a "lovely figure" and be "beautiful": Rachel and Esther (Gen. 29:17 and Esther 2:7, respectively). Each lover in the Song of Solomon is described in similar terms, as in "His mouth is sweetness itself; he is altogether lovely" (5:16) and "You are as beautiful as Tirzah, my darling, as lovely as Jerusalem" (6:4).

When the psalmist exclaims, "How lovely is your dwelling place, Lord Almighty" (84:1), the meaning primarily seems to be that the temple is lovely because the Lord is present there. This also seems to be the meaning of another Psalm, which says, "One thing I ask from the Lord, this only do I seek: that I may dwell in the house of the Lord all the days of my life, to gaze on the beauty of the Lord and to seek him in his temple" (27:4).

The temple was, in fact, a beautiful place, and that beauty, like the one Suger extolled in his day, would no doubt have helped worshipers sense the presence of God. In 1 Kings, we get a glimpse of the temple's ornamentation:

> Solomon covered the inside of the temple with pure gold, and he extended gold chains across the front of the inner sanctuary, which was overlaid with gold. . . . He also overlaid with gold the altar that belonged to the inner sanctuary. . . .
>
> He placed the cherubim inside the innermost room of the temple, with their wings spread out. The wing of one cherub touched one wall, while the wing of the other touched the other wall, and their wings touched each other in the middle of the room. He overlaid the cherubim with gold.
>
> On the walls all around the temple, in both the inner and outer rooms, he carved cherubim, palm trees, and open

flowers. He also covered the floors of both the inner and outer rooms of the temple with gold. (6:21–30)

Solomon took his cues from the divine instructions in Exodus about how to build the tabernacle. God commanded Bezalel, whom the Lord has gifted, "to make artistic designs for work in gold, silver, and bronze" (31:4). Curtains were made of "blue, purple, and scarlet yarn and finely twisted linen, with cherubim woven into it by a skilled worker," who is later described as an "embroiderer" (36:35, 37). The cover for the ark was made of "pure gold," with "two cherubim out of hammered gold at the ends of the cover" (37:6–7).

Apparently the Lord's command, "You shall not make for yourself an image in the form of anything in heaven above or on the earth beneath or in the waters below" (20:4), did not fully apply to the building of the tabernacle and later, the temple. If such images could help uplift the soul to the true God, they were to be used.

The ancient Israelites understood a common human experience: beauty takes us out of ourselves, even out of our world. It is transcendent. It prompts us to ponder spiritual realities, to think about God.

BEAUTY CALLS US HIGHER

In his article "The Problem of Beauty," author Matt Woodley says, "British philosopher Roger Scruton wrote, '[Beauty] is never viewed with indifference. Beauty demands to be noticed; it speaks to us directly like the voice of an intimate friend.' When we are attuned to the beauty around us, it should prompt us to say, 'Whom do I thank for this?'"[21]

Woodley also points out a command hidden in a verse that we normally associate only with worry: "Consider the lilies of the field, how they grow: they neither toil nor spin, yet I tell you, even Solomon in all his glory was not arrayed like one of these" (Matt. 6:28–29, ESV).

The Greek word behind the imperative here is stronger than *consider*. It means "observe" or "consider closely." Jesus is commanding us to behold the beauty of the earth; that will prompt us to think about God, and that in turn will calm our worry.

It is no surprise, then, that recent social science research finds a link between beauty and happiness. Cody C. Delistraty, in an *Atlantic* article, "The Beauty-Happiness Connection," writes,

> The usual markers of happiness are colloquially known as the "Big Seven:" wealth (especially compared to those around you), family relationships, career, friends, health, freedom, and personal values, as outlined by London School of Economics professor Richard Layard in *Happiness: Lessons from a New Science*. According to the Goldberg study, however, what makes people happiest isn't even in the Big Seven. Instead, happiness is most easily attained by living in an aesthetically beautiful city.

He goes on to say that when people are embedded in beauty—"lovely architecture, history, green spaces, cobblestone streets"—they are happier. Delistraty says the study shows that "the cumulative positive effects of daily beauty worked subtly but strongly."[22]

Happiness is a far cry from transcendence, but it may be the first small step in that direction. The beauty of the natural world certainly made theologian Jonathan Edwards happy, and so much more:

> when we are delighted with flowery meadows and gentle breezes of wind, we may consider that we only see the emanations of the sweet benevolence of Jesus Christ; when we behold the fragrant rose and lily, we see his love and purity. So the green trees and fields, and singing of birds, are emanations of his infinite joy and benignity; the easiness and naturalness of trees and vines [are] shadows of his infinite beauty and loveliness; the crystal rivers and murmuring streams have the footsteps of his

sweet grace and bounty.[23]

For Edwards, beauty was a picture of the grace and loveliness of Jesus. This is one reason the Catholic Church, under Pope Benedict XVI, believed that beauty should be at the heart of evangelism today. "I have often affirmed my conviction," he wrote, "that the true apology of Christian faith, the most convincing demonstration of its truth . . . are the saints and the beauty that the faith has generated." Benedict XVI talked about *via pulchritudinis,* the way of beauty, long before he became pope. In a post-Christian world that is unreceptive to the church, Benedict found that the message of beauty is a crucial element in presenting the gospel to an unbelieving world.[24] He cited C. S. Lewis when making this point, who believed that beauty incites a desire to join infinite Beauty, which beauty can only reflect.[25]

It's not that beauty will lead immediately to an apprehension of God's love for us in Jesus Christ—but if we take beauty seriously, it can do that. According to Edwards, "God is God, and distinguished from all other beings, and exalted above 'em, chiefly by his divine beauty."[26] Thus any beauty we experience reflects, however faintly, the being of God.

In our pragmatic age, we are tempted to imagine that beauty is a luxury, a pleasant addition to our otherwise busy and efficient lives of doing good and pursuing truth. Instead, it turns out that it is just as essential to the Christian life as is goodness and truth—Edwards would argue that it is most essential. We can let the theologians argue that out, while we simply affirm that beauty is an essential ingredient to that which I'm calling Beautiful Orthodoxy.

CHAPTER 6

UNCOMMON BEAUTY

I f the pursuit of the good can lead to moralism, and the pursuit of truth to pride, so an inordinate attention to beauty can lead to idolatry. This is the paradox of beauty. In the previous chapter, we gave many examples of how beauty can lead us to God; sadly, beauty can also lead us to false gods.

This is one reason certain branches of Christianity have remained suspicious of beauty. The Reformed are especially concerned to exalt the singularity of God, and they have highly sensitive antennae that pick up the slight hints of idolatry. They come by their righteous jealousy for God honestly, as Moses warned the people of Israel:

> Therefore watch yourselves very carefully, so that you do not become corrupt and make for yourselves an idol, an image of any shape, whether formed like a man or a woman, or like any animal on earth or any bird that flies in the air, or like any creature that moves along the ground or

any fish in the waters below. And when you look up to the sky and see the sun, the moon, and the stars—all the heavenly array—do not be enticed into bowing down to them and worshiping things the Lord your God has apportioned to all the nations under heaven. (Deut. 4:15–19)

The created world—so beautiful as it is, so reflective of the glory of God—tempts weak human minds to be "enticed into bowing down . . . and worshiping" the creation itself. So common is this, the apostle Paul considers it the root of our alienation from God, when we "exchanged the glory of the immortal God for images" (Rom. 1:23).

We may not be tempted in our age to worship literal idols made of human hands, but we are tempted to idolize beauty, both manmade and God-made. We can become so enraptured with it, that we are apt to mimic Henry Thoreau's famous line about wildness and say, "In beauty is the preservation of the world." To the extent that the beautification of our homes and gardens, and our exultation in the natural beauty of creation, leads us to God, all is to the good. To the extent that it tempts us to seek the pleasure of beauty as an end in itself, it's not so good: "When the woman saw that the fruit of the tree was good for food and pleasing to the eye . . . she took some and ate it" (Gen. 3:6).

Penultimate beauty is the gift of God that makes us feel good. Recall the definition from the previous chapter: "the quality or aggregate of qualities in a person or thing that gives pleasure to the senses or pleasurably exalts the mind or spirit: loveliness."[27] Most of us would have a difficult time living without this type of beauty, that is, in poverty or destitution. And so we are willing to spend our hard-earned money on our homes, cars, clothes, and vacations so we can surround ourselves with beauty. To be bereft of feel-good beauty leaves us despondent and irritable. We may even find ourselves saying that we just cannot be happy without some beauty in our lives, and that is likely true in a limited sense.

THE GREATEST BEAUTY

Ultimate beauty, however, is not about the experience of pleasure as such. Ultimate beauty drills into us more deeply, prompting not pleasure as much as awe, which can include fear and wonder. It is the *mysterium tremendum et fascinans*, a mystery that fascinates us yet also makes us tremble. It may not, in fact, be pleasurable to behold.

Jesus Christ on the cross would be the supreme example. There is nothing pleasurable about this picture. It does not accord with any standards of loveliness as we have understood and experienced them. It is a gruesome and ghastly picture. "He had no beauty or majesty to attract us to him, nothing in his appearance that we should desire him" (Isa. 53:2).

If one turns away from a crucifix or crucifixion painting feeling a surge of pleasure, something is terribly wrong, either with the artist's rendition or the state of one's soul. It is not "beautiful" by our standard reckoning. That's why some consider a 1987 photograph by the American artist and photographer Andres Serrano as blasphemy. The picture shows a small plastic crucifix in a glass of the artist's urine. Many Christians found it offensive, the desecration of a sacred religious symbol. Some were so angry they attempted to wield hammers against it.

It is indeed offensive and repulsive at many levels, but perhaps we can see why that repulsion might be just the point. The crucifixion was where the One who is truly innocent and holy died a sinner's death on a shameful cross.

But do we not believe also that the crucifixion was beautiful in the deepest sense of the word? That is, "lovely" in the sense that it is the ultimate picture of love? Does it not make us tremble with both remorse at our sin and repulsion at the suffering of the Son of God? Does it not lead to renewed repentance and fresh forgiveness? Does it not cast us down in humiliation and lift us up to the shining mountain of transfiguration? Does it not allow us to enter into the mystery of death and the mystery of life, a life Jesus calls "eternal" and whom he says is nothing less than participation in him, the life, the dying and rising One (John 14:6)?

That's ultimate beauty. This is why in the Gospel of John, the crucifixion is the ultimate manifestation of God's glory—it is the hour that the Son of Man is glorified (12:27–28). *Glory* is a word normally associated with great beauty and splendor, but here it points something closer to fearsome magnificence.

We see other examples of this beauty in the saints. One of the most memorable scenes in the life of St. Francis is this one as described in *The Legend of the Three Companions*:

> One day while Francis was praying fervently to God, he received an answer: "O Francis, if you want to know my will, you must hate and despise all that which hitherto your body has loved and desired to possess. Once you begin to do this, all that formerly seemed sweet and pleasant to you will become bitter and unbearable, and instead, the things that formerly made you shudder will bring you great sweetness and content." Francis was divinely comforted and greatly encouraged by these words.

God's call on his life is in one sense to eschew beauty, that which to Francis had seemed "sweet and pleasant." The story continues:

> Then one day, as he was riding near Assisi, he met a leper. He had always felt an overpowering horror of these sufferers, but making a great effort, he conquered his aversion, dismounted, and, in giving the leper a coin, kissed his hand. The leper then gave him the kiss of peace, after which Francis remounted his horse and rode on his way.
>
> Some days later he took a large sum of money to the leper hospital, and gathering all the inmates together, he gave them alms, kissing each of their hands. Formerly he could

neither touch [nor] even look at lepers, but when he left them on that day, what had been so repugnant to him had really and truly been turned into something pleasant.

Indeed, his previous aversion to lepers had been so strong, that, besides being incapable of looking at them, he would not even approach the places where they lived. And if by chance he happened to pass anywhere near their dwellings or to see one of the lepers, even though he was moved to give them an alms through some intermediate person, he would nevertheless turn his face away and hold his nose. But, strengthened by God's grace, he was enabled to obey the command and to love what he had hated and to abhor what he had hitherto wrongfully loved.[28]

The story does not say it directly, or say it like we would these days, but Francis perceived the *imago dei* in the unfortunate and horribly disfigured: people with skin sores and lumps; whose loss of physical feeling led to loss of fingers and toes. What in outward appearance was ugly was in fact nonetheless something beautiful—and it took a kiss for Francis to see it.

But also note what happens to us as we mentally view this scene. The picture of Francis kissing a leper repulses us as well. To watch him makes us wince. And yet we recognize that he is doing something beautiful for God.

DIVINE BEAUTY

Today, we associate the phrase of doing something beautiful for God with Mother Teresa. She was by no means a beautiful woman to behold, especially in her later years when she was most well known. Stooped over and wrinkled with age, she was a complete contrast to lovely Princess Diana, to whom she is often contrasted because both humanitarians died on the same day. Neither was the iconic picture of Mother Teresa beautiful, kneeling next to a dying man from the streets of Kolkata, a man crucified by life, breathing his last. We see an uncomely woman feeding wasted men and women—yet we recognize a picture of someone doing "something beautiful for God." This became the title of Malcolm Muggeridge's book about the saint.

The careful reader, like a philosopher friend of mine, will rightly suspect me of mixing categories. Jesus, Francis, and Mother Teresa are examples of moral goodness, even ultimate goodness since they performed acts of mercy. One could also argue that they speak of ultimate truth, meaning they point to the most basic reality of the universe: that it is grounded and enveloped in love and mercy. And yet such acts get frozen in our minds, either from the art they inspire or the photographs that are framed. And they become, in that sense, works of art, art at its most beautiful. This is in part because of the skill of the artist or photographer, but mostly because of the subject matter at hand.

This is not a new insight. For the ancient philosopher Plato, beauty was "the splendor of truth" (the title of John Paul II's famous encyclical). Plato, in his *Symposium,* argues that beauty is a close cousin to the Good. All three are transcendental attributes of what he considered the divine essence. For Plato physical manifestations of earthly beauty imitate divine beauty. Paintings, sculptures, and so forth are but "imitations of imitations." The true artist, when divinely inspired, can help us perceive pure beauty or "divine goodness" in much the same way as an inspired philosopher can help us grasp "divine truth." A modern-day realist philosopher comes to the same conclusion: Catholic Josef Pieper, wrote, "Beauty is the glow of the true and the good that shines forth from every ordered state of being."[29]

That which is good is also truthful and beautiful. That which is truthful is also good and beautiful. And that which is beautiful is also good and truthful. In the end, there is no hard and fast way to separate goodness, truth, and beauty, any more than one can separate Father, Son, and Holy Spirit. To paraphrase the Chalcedon Definition, a fifth-century document which sought to understand the relationship of Jesus to the Father: we recognize these "transcendentals" as having three natures, "without confusion ... without division, without separation; the distinction of natures being in no way annulled by the union, but rather the characteristics of each nature being preserved and coming together to form one."[30]

The weaving of goodness, truth, and beauty is what sits at the core of the phrase *Beautiful Orthodoxy*. We seek to pursue goodness and truth (again, orthodoxy in its fullest sense is about both) that is beautiful. We pursue beauty not in a merely aesthetic sense, but ultimately as a sign of eternal life, that quality of life full of the goodness and truth of Jesus Christ.

EPILOGUE

What's left, of course, is to sketch examples of what the good, the true, and the beautiful look like. In one sense, books have already been written about this: biographies of the saints, inspirational stories of missionaries and heroes of social justice. But we must note—in each section that follows—both the extraordinary and ordinary examples, those that encompass the world and those that speak to us as individuals.

THE GOOD

We've already noted a few small and large examples of the good (especially that of Nelson Mandela). Examples of everyday good abound: from refusing to participate in the shaming culture of social media, to doing the dishes for one's spouse, to letting a stranger in line ahead of you, to making it a habit of saying "please" and "thank you." In short, for treating people as we would have them treat us. And then sometimes going the extra mile of lending without expecting a return, volunteering at the homeless shelter, or taking a wayward relative into your home. This basic common good is important not only for the smooth running of society, but also as a way of letting our neighbors taste little bits of grace.

But we must not mistake the good for the merely nice, seeing our calling "to do good to all people" as akin to not ruffling feathers. Some of the finest human beings upset the social order when it became oppressive, even using coercion to put things right. As Reinhold Niebuhr argued eloquently in *Moral Man and Immoral Society*, even "nonviolence does coerce."[31] Martin Luther King Jr., in his civil rights efforts, understood this better than most:

> Nonviolent direct action seeks to create such a crisis and foster such a tension that a community which has constantly refused to negotiate is forced to confront the issue. It seeks so to dramatize the issue that it can no longer be ignored. My citing the creation of tension as part of the work of the nonviolent resister may sound rather shocking. But I must confess that I am not afraid of the word "tension."[32]

So doing the good on behalf of the Good will entail actions from common courtesy to social action, from being hospitable to strangers to discomforting the unjustly comfortable.

THE TRUE

Truth, like goodness, touches nearly every aspect of our lives. It begins in teaching children not to lie, a lesson that some of our church leaders and highest government officials never seem to learn. In an age in which trust of leaders, spiritual and secular, is at an all-time low, how refreshing it would be for Christians to be known as people of their word. Jesus talks about this as our yes being yes, and our no being no. A good sign that we're fudging on the truth is when we simply cannot say yes or no, but feel the need to explain ourselves. In politics, it's called spinning the truth. But when you get down to it, it's just bearing false witness.

Other examples of truth telling lie in the area of evangelism and apologetics. A friend tells the story of his attempt to argue his college classmates into the Christian faith. In a class on world religions, he and some friends gave what he believed was an unassailable apologetic for Christianity as a class presentation. During the discussion afterward, it became clear that the non-Christians were either bored or hostile, despite what he felt was the superior logic of the Christian view. Only years later did my friend grasp that while he may have presented the abstract truths of Christianity cogently, he had failed to also present the person of Jesus Christ in a way that conveyed that our faith is first and foremost an intimate encounter with the living God, who is Truth.

When we don't frame our apologetics or theology with the personal dimension in play, our talk about Christ is not *fully* true, let alone attractive. Our theology is also not fully true if we fail to embed it in the grand story of Scripture, which is nothing less than the greatest love story ever told. This is what novelist Dorothy Sayers was getting at in her essay, "The Greatest Drama Ever Staged":

> That God should play the tyrant over man is a dismal story of unrelieved oppression; that man should play the tyrant over man is the usual dreary record of human futility; but that man should play the tyrant over God and find him a better man than himself is an astonishing drama indeed. Any journalist, hearing of it for the first time, would recognize it as news; those who did hear it for the first time actually called it news, and good news at that; though we are likely to forget that the word Gospel ever meant anything so sensational.[33]

For our evangelism and teaching to be true in the deepest sense, it must stick close to the personal Truth that is Jesus Christ, and the personal and dramatic story of Genesis to Revelation.

THE BEAUTIFUL

Discussion about practical examples of pursuing the beautiful must begin in Genesis 1. We have been handed a beautiful world of sky and seas, of "seed-bearing plants and trees . . . [of] various kinds," of "living creatures" of the sea and "birds [that] fly above the earth" and "all the creatures that move along the ground." When God casts his eye over everything he had made, especially man and woman, he called it all "very good." In other words, he "made every beautiful thing in its time" (Ecc. 3:11), and all creation is intended for our pleasure and for the glory of God (Ps. 19).

But we live in an industrial and technological age committed to unbounded growth. We are tempted to level forests and pave meadows and dry up rivers and cloud the air for the sake of economic growth and economic efficiency. Christians should be shocked and appalled at the desecration of creation, throwing themselves in front of the juggernaut, pleading on behalf of voiceless creation. This is not just for the sake of wondrous creation, but for the sake of humanity, who without a glorious creation will have less chance of beholding a glorious Creator.

That's one grand social dimension of our calling to pursue and protect beauty, but there are small and significant ways as well. Few guys' college dorms are known for their beauty, but I still recall fondly what happened in my dorm when a graduate student, who happened to be a Christian, moved in. He made it a point to place a vase of flowers on a table just to the left of the entrance to our hallway. It was a small thing, but I was surprised how it positively shaped my feelings when I stepped into the otherwise drab institutional corridor. It was a small but significant witness to "the beauty of the earth" we are called to exult in.

Beauty can have an extraordinary effect on us, sometimes leading to the turning around of a wayward life. The famous monk Thomas

Merton was a profligate and cynical young man, but slowly found himself turning around. On a trip to Rome, he began visiting churches for their art, which led him to the Gospels they portrayed so beautifully. Slowly, he says,

> I read more and more of the Gospels, and my love for the old churches and their mosaics grew from day to day. Soon I was no longer visiting them merely for the art. There was something else that attracted me: a kind of interior peace. I loved to be in these holy places. I had a kind of deep and strong conviction that I belonged there.[34]

He later said he "had almost discovered the divinity of Christ in the ancient mosaics of the churches of Rome."[35]

This story suggests a powerful role for the Christian artist. Not that Christian artists are confined to religious themes. Makoto Fujimura is perhaps the most well-known Christian artist today, and he expresses his art in abstract paintings that often have no obvious religious or biblical theme. And yet in, with, and under his paintings, one can sense a Christian sensibility. He expressed this succinctly in his acceptance speech for the 2014 Religion and the Arts Award. He had just quoted an Emily Dickinson poem that in one stanza read:

> "Hope" is the thing with feathers -
> That perches in the soul -
> And sings the tune without the words -
> And never stops - at all -

Fujimura comments,

> Art and poetry are a "thing with feathers" that awakens us to the inevitable reality of our senses, the aroma of the new. But we must learn to see, hear, and feel beyond our senses: We must learn to see with the "eyes of our heart."... To see with the eyes of the heart so that we may

know hope: that is what is required of us today.[36]

He is of course referring to St. Paul's prayer, "I pray that the eyes of your heart may be enlightened in order that you may know the hope to which he has called you, the riches of his glorious inheritance in his holy people" (Eph. 1:18). The Christian artist, no matter the theme or medium employed, is to help any and every one, even when despair is most profound, to sense a hope that transcends this world. When they do that, of course, they have moved beyond beauty as that which gives us pleasure, onto the uncommon beauty that mysteriously instills awe and wonder.

As noted in the last chapter, it's not always easy to separate the good, the true, and the beautiful because they so often appear together. Mandela's goodness was also true in the deepest sense, and beautiful to behold. A finely crafted argument or proof—whether that be in theology, philosophy, or mathematics—is said to be elegant, a thing of beauty, and thus good. A Fujimura abstract is certainly beautiful and as such also true. Whenever and wherever we find goodness, truth, and beauty falling over one another, we are likely to spot the Good, True, and Beautiful One.

THE PARADOX OF BEAUTIFUL ORTHODOXY

Yet it isn't as if we have to wait around for extraordinary moments to experience this triune wonder. The Good, True, and Beautiful One also makes himself known also in the most prosaic of ways—in his church.

"[W]here two or three are gathered in my name," said Jesus, "there am I am among them" (Matt. 18:20, ESV). This is generally interpreted to mean that when Christians gather for prayer and worship, Christ is especially present. But the apostle Paul is more specific. He ties the presence of Christ to two actions the church takes in worship.

The first is an act by which one becomes part of the church; that is, the body of Christ as it is present in the world:

> For we were all baptized by one Spirit so as to form one
> body—whether Jews or Gentiles, slave or free—and we
> were all given the one Spirit to drink. . . . Now you are
> the body of Christ, and each one of you is a part of it. (1
> Cor. 12:13, 27)

The other act is in one sense a continual renewal of our baptism:

> The cup of blessing which we bless, is it not a participa-
> tion in the blood of Christ? The bread that we break, is it
> not a participation in the body of Christ? Because there
> is one bread, we who are many are one body, for we all
> partake of the one bread. (1 Cor. 10:16–17, ESV)

One does not have to be an Anglican or an Orthodox or a Catholic to
take such language with utmost seriousness. Baptist Charles Spurgeon
believed that to participate in the Lord's Supper was to encounter the
resurrected Christ:

> At all times when you come to the Communion table,
> count it to have been no ordinance of grace to you unless
> you have gone right through the veil into Christ's own
> arms, or at least have touched his garment, feeling that
> the first object, the life and soul of the means of grace, is
> to touch Jesus Christ himself.[37]

Christians differ about what happens in the Lord's Supper, from the
bread and wine becoming the body and blood by the words of institu-
tion, to Christ being received in the bread and wine by the faith of the
individual believer. But few Christians deny the special presence of
Christ in this act of worship.

The other moment in worship when Christ is found is preaching.
Jesus put it succinctly when he commissioned his disciples to
preach: "He who hears you hears me" (Luke 10:16). The church has

taken this to mean that when the Word of God is preached, the Word of God is preaching.

This was understood from the beginning. The church father Augustine said, "The preacher explains the text; if he says what is true, it is Christ speaking."[38] We find the idea repeated in other church fathers, in the Reformers, and to this day, in teachers like J. I. Packer:

> A true sermon is an act of God, and not a mere performance by man. In real preaching the speaker is the servant of the Word and God speaks and works by the Word through his servant's lips. . . . The sermon . . . is God's ordained means of speaking and working.[39]

In all sorts of ways—baptism, preaching, and the Lord's Supper—Christ is especially present in his church. But here is the rub: Anyone who has spent any time in a local church would hardly describe the church as the epitome of Beautiful Orthodoxy. The church is not so much a lived experience of the good, the true, and the beautiful as much as the disappointing manifestation of the sinful, the confused, and the unseemly.

It's at just this point that we are called to look beyond the penultimate good, the penultimate true, and the penultimate beauty. We need to look beyond ourselves when we look at the church if we're going to see the gracious miracle that it is.

If ultimate goodness is mercy to the sinner, then the church is an expression of ultimate goodness. For what else is it but a sinful body with whom Christ is mercifully present? And if ultimate truth is the person of Christ himself, then the church is an expression of ultimate truth. Has not Jesus promised to give himself to it? If ultimate beauty is the kissing of despised lepers, is not the church an expression of ultimate beauty, for does not Christ kiss and serve us spiritual lepers in worship?

If we think of the church primarily as what *we* do, of course, the church is anything but beautiful or orthodox. It falls oh so short of the good, the true, and the beautiful day in, day out. But if we recall that the church is called into being by Jesus Christ, and lives and moves and breathes by his presence, then the church is nothing less than a daily and miraculous sign of the good, the true, and the beautiful.

We *are* redeemed even though we don't always looked redeemed. We nonetheless strive to become what we are. In the same way, we may not always exemplify the good, the true, and the beautiful, but we *are* good, true, and beautiful because we are one in union with Christ. This merciful reality, saturated in grace, is what drives us to make Beautiful Orthodoxy a living presence in our churches and in our world.

ENDNOTES

[1] Nick English, "Anger Is the Internet's Most Powerful Emotion," *USA Today* online, September 24, 2013: http://www.usatoday.com/story/news/nation/2013/09/24/anger-internet-most-powerful-emotion/2863869/.

[2] Natalie Wolchover, "Why Is Everyone on the Internet So Angry?" *Scientific American* online, July 25, 2012: http://www.scientificamerican.com/article/why-is-everyone-on-the-internet-so-angry/.

[3] Rabbi David Wolpe, "Why Americans Are So Angry About Everything," *Time* online, January 5, 2016: http://time.com/4166326/why-americans-are-so-angry-about-everything/.

[4] Rollo May, *My Quest for Beauty*, (Dallas: Saybrook, 1985), 20.

[5] Robert Fulghum, *All I Really Need to Know I Learned in Kindergarten*, rev. ed. (New York: Ballantine Books, 2004), 2–3.

[6] "How to Live the Good Life," Elite Daily, last modified January 11, 2013:

http://elitedaily.com/life/motivation/live-good-life/.

[7] Justin Lear and Dorrine Mendoza, "5 examples of humans being amazing," CNN, October 26, 2013: http://www.cnn.com/2013/10/25/us/5-examples-of-humans-being-amazing/.

[8] David Brooks, "If It Feels Right . . . " *The New York Times*, September 12, 2011: http://www.nytimes.com/2011/09/13/opinion/if-it-feels-right.html.

[9] Kharunya Paramaguru, "5 Great Stories About Nelson Mandela's Humility, Kindness, and Courage," *Time*, December 6, 2013: http://world.time.com/2013/12/06/5-great-stories-about-nelson-mandelas-humility-kindness-and-courage/.

[10] *The Long Walk of Nelson Mandela: Anecdotes and Insights*, FRONTLINE, published May 1999, accessed August 29, 2016: http://www.pbs.org/wgbh/pages/frontline/shows/mandela/etc/insights.html.

[11] Faith Karimi, "Nelson Mandela, anti-apartheid icon and father of modern South Africa, dies," CNN, December 5, 2013: http://www.cnn.com/2013/12/05/world/africa/nelson-mandela/.

[12] Among the many summaries readily available that summarize the major lines of interpretation, I found these particularly helpful: Harvey K. McArthur's *Understanding the Sermon on the Mount* (New York: Harper, 1960) outlines the leading views up to his day. Scot McKnight's *Sermon on the Mount* (Grand Rapids: Zondervan, 2013) discusses more recent interpretations.

[13] "Why the Cross: The Reason Jesus Chose to Die a Bloody, Horrible Death," an interview with Fleming Rutledge by Mark Galli, *Christianity Today*, March 2016: http://www.christianitytoday.com/ct/2016/march/why-did-jesus-choose-cross.html.

[14] "Venerable Sisoes the Great," on the Orthodox Church in America website, last modified July 6, 2013: https://oca.org/saints/lives/2013/07/06/101918-venerable-sisoes-the-great.

[15] Thomas Paine, *The Age of Reason: Being an Investigation of True and Fabulous Theology,* (New York: G. Putnam and Sons, 1896), 184.

[16] Christopher Hitchens, *Letters to a Young Contrarian,* (New York: Basic Books, 2005), 58.

[17] Steve Taylor, "Dogmatic and Spiritual Religion," *Out of the Darkness* (blog), *Psychology Today,* December 19, 2014: https://www.psychologytoday.com/blog/out-the-darkness/201412/dogmatic-and-spiritual-religion.

[18] Gregory of Nyssa, as quoted by Paul Evdokimov in *Orthodoxy: The Cosmos Transfigured* (Kansas City: Eighth Day Press, 2012), translated by Anthony P. Gytheil. The ideas in the paragraph are indebted to this book, pp. 49–52.

[19] Hamilton Reed Armstrong, "Art, Beauty, & Imagination - A Catholic Perspective," A.G. Dei (website), accessed August 29, 2016: http://agdei.com/Art&Beauty2.html.

[20] *Merriam-Webster Online,* s.v. "beauty," accessed August 29, 2016: http://www.merriam-webster.com/dictionary/beauty.

[21] Matt Woodley, "The Problem with Beauty," *Behemoth,* Issue 17, March 5, 2015: http://www.christianitytoday.com/behemoth/2015/issue-17/problem-of-beauty.html.

[22] Cody C. Delistraty, "The Beauty-Happiness Connection," *The Atlantic,* August 15, 2014: http://www.theatlantic.com/health/archive/2014/08/the-beautyhappiness-connection/375678/.

[23] Belden C. Lane, "Jonathan Edwards on Beauty, Desire, and the Sensory World," *Theological Studies* 65 (2004): 51. http://cdn.theologicalstudies.net/65/65.1/65.1.3.pdf.

[24] Matthew J. Ramage, "Pope Benedict XVI's Theology of Beauty and the New Evangelization," *Homiletic & Pastoral Review* (January 29, 2015): http://www.hprweb.com/2015/01/pope-benedict-xvis-theology-of-beauty-and-the-new-evangelization/.

[25] Ibid.

[26] Belden C. Lane, "Jonathan Edwards on Beauty, Desire, and the Sensory World," *Theological Studies* 65 (2004): 51. http://cdn.theologicalstudies.net/65/65.1/65.1.3.pdf.

[27] *Merriam-Webster Online*, s.v. "beauty," accessed August 29, 2016: http://www.merriam-webster.com/dictionary/beauty.

[28] "Meet St. Francis," Christian History, last modified August 2008: http://www.christianitytoday.com/history/2008/august/meet-st-francis.html?share=Va7vGcVJY%2b0leZUV7p%2bfUMjg7dtOub1e.

[29] Hamilton Reed Armstrong, "Is 'Beauty' an objective reality or only in the eye of the beholder?" *Fellowship of Catholic Scholars Quarterly*, no. 1 (Winter 2009): http://agdei.com/beautyandbeholder.html.

[30] Chalcedon Definition, accessed August 30, 2016: http://www.reformed.org/documents/index.html?mainframe=http://www.reformed.org/documents/chalcedon.html.

[31] Reinhold Niebuhr, *Moral Man and Immoral Society* (Louisville: Westminster John Knox Press, 1932), 241.

[32] Martin Luther King Jr., "Letter from a Birmingham Jail" (April 16, 1963): https://www.africa.upenn.edu/Articles_Gen/Letter_Birmingham.html.

[33] "Dorothy Sayers: Theology Is Thrilling (The Dogma Is the Drama!)", *Bible Mesh Blog*, February 11, 2014: https://biblemesh.com/blog/sayers-theology-is-thrilling-the-dogma-is-the-drama/.

[34] Thomas Merton, *The Seven Storey Mountain*, rev. ed. (New York: Mariner Books, 1999), 122.

[35] Ibid., 229.

[36] Makoto Fujimura, "Toward Culture Care" (speech, San Diego,

November 23, 2014), posted November 27, 2014: http://www.
makotofujimura.com/writings-toward-culture-care-2014-religion-and-
the-arts-award-acceptance-speech/.

[37] Charles Spurgeon, *Till He Come* (1896): http://www.ccel.org/ccel/spur-
geon/till_he_come.xviii.html.

[38] "Christ Speaking Through Preaching," Covenant Protestant Reformed
Church, accessed August 29, 2016: http://www.cprf.co.uk/quotes/christ-
speakingpreaching.htm#.V7b8h46-jwM.

[39] Ibid.